The Pigeon with the Silver Foot

By Pamela Hansford Johnson and
C.P. Snow

WWW.SAMUELFRENCH.CO.UK
WWW.SAMUELFRENCH.COM

Copyright © 1956 by Pamela Hansford Johnson and C.P. Snow
Reprinted 1967
All Rights Reserved

THE PIGEON WITH THE SILVER FOOT is fully protected under the copyright laws of the British Commonwealth, including Canada, the United States of America, and all other countries of the Copyright Union. All rights, including professional and amateur stage productions, recitation, lecturing, public reading, motion picture, radio broadcasting, television and the rights of translation into foreign languages are strictly reserved.

ISBN 978-0-573-12004-6

www.samuelfrench-london.co.uk

www.samuelfrench.com

For Amateur Production Enquiries

United Kingdom and World excluding north america

plays@SamuelFrench-London.co.uk

020 7255 4302/01

Each title is subject to availability from Samuel French,

depending upon country of performance.

CAUTION: Professional and amateur producers are hereby warned that THE PIGEON WITH THE SILVER FOOT is subject to a licensing fee. Publication of this play does not imply availability for performance. Both amateurs and professionals considering a production are strongly advised to apply to the appropriate agent before starting rehearsals, advertising, or booking a theatre. A licensing fee must be paid whether the title is presented for charity or gain and whether or not admission is charged.

The professional rights in this play are controlled by Samuel French Ltd, 52 Fitzroy Street, London, W1T 5JR

No one shall make any changes in this title for the purpose of production. No part of this book may be reproduced, stored in a retrieval system, or transmitted in any form, by any means, now known or yet to be invented, including mechanical, electronic, photocopying, recording, videotaping, or otherwise, without the prior written permission of the publisher. No one shall upload this title, or part of this title, to any social media websites.

The right of Pamela Hansford Johnson and C.P. Snow to be identified as author of this work has been asserted in accordance with Section 77 of the Copyright, Designs and Patents Act 1988.

© *Pamela Hansford Johnson and C. P. Snow*
Reprinted 1967

INTRODUCTION

The charm of this play is bound up largely with the charm of presentation. Take trouble with your set, and achieve good proportion and good colours. Vivify the scene with bright café chairs, and a single splash of splendid colour in BIANCA's home.

Rehearse your spot-lighting carefully, and cross-fade the lights gently. Make sure your gelatines *add* to the atmosphere of each scene, and do not "kill" the general colour-scheme. Perhaps pink would light the café best, straw for BIANCA's room, and steel for the street scenes. But whatever scheme you decide on, discuss it with a lighting expert and with your décor artist, so that you finally achieve a harmonious effect.

The miming is all important, too. If it is clumsy or self-conscious, your production will be ruined. Cast an artist who naturally moves and walks well, and then bring in the dance teacher to help you out!

CHARACTERS

4 women
2 men
3 singers

Of today	*Of yesterday*
MARY	BIANCA
JOANNA	MARIO
THE WAITER AT FLORIAN'S	THE CUSTOMER
* * *	THE BEGGAR (to be doubled by the CUSTOMER)
2 or 3 female voices to sing	
2 torchbearers (optional)	THE LOVER (to be doubled by MARIO)

SCENE: *The piazza San Marco, in Venice*
TIME: *The present*

*THE PIGEON WITH THE SILVER FOOT

SCENE: *The Piazza San Marco, in Venice. This may be suggested by a row of five arches with a round lamp at each. The arches should stand in front of a dark backcloth or curtain, and the interiors of all except the middle should be blocked in. (See illustration on page twenty-four.) In front of the arch, to the extreme* L., *a few yellow tables and chairs, representing* FLORIAN'S *café.*

When the curtain rises, only the L. *of the stage is lit. At the end of the modern scene, this should be plunged in darkness, and the light turned upon the centre arch, which should be hollowed out to reveal a small inset scene, representing the home of* BIANCA, *the lacemaker. There need be no more in this room than a bed, a table and a chair: lace should be lying about. It is important that when the interior scenes are over, this arch should be blacked out completely.*

The curtain rises on the Present: the time is near midnight on the Piazza San Marco, late October. The two girls, MARY *and* JOANNA, *just out of their teens, are sitting over their ice-creams outside* FLORIAN'S. MARY *is slender, fair and rather gentle.* JOANNA *is dark, handsome and stalwart, obviously the one who arranges travel and pays the bills.*

The WAITER *is fidgeting around the table, flicking at the top, changing an ashtray, sometimes looking at his watch.*

MARY *is whistling softly to herself.*

JOANNA. What's that you're whistling?
MARY. Whistling? Oh . . . I think it was something I heard this morning. One of the gondoliers was humming it.
JOANNA. It's pretty. I wonder what the words are.
MARY. Do you think it's a song?

NOTE: *All stage directions are given from the point of view of the audience.*

* It is illegal to perform this play, *in any circumstances whatsoever*, without a licence. Please refer, for full details, to Copyright Notice on page two of cover.

JOANNA. Oh, of course. You can almost hear the words that go with it. I wish I could hear them.
(MARY *goes on whistling, very softly and sweetly.*
The WAITER *takes a look at both girls, begins to stack remaining chairs and tables.*)
I am glad we decided to make it Venice!
MARY. So am I. I think it must be more beautiful now, in late autumn, even if there aren't so many people about.
JOANNA. It was an awful business saving up, wasn't it?
MARY. But worth it.
JOANNA. We shall be as poor as church mice for the rest of the year.
MARY. I don't care. You know (*Dreamily.*) I shall never forget this: sitting outside Florian's, where Lord Byron used to sit, looking at the moon shining on Saint Mark's.
JOANNA. We could do with a Byron, I suppose. Perhaps one ought to have a romance in Venice. There's something missing, really, for two girls travelling alone.
(*The* WAITER *has returned to lean against one of the arches. He listens, smiling, to this exchange.*)
MARY. We're young. There's plenty of time for us.
JOANNA. Sometimes I think we're just superfluous women.
MARY. Oh, come! Neither of us is twenty-two yet!
JOANNA (*gloomily*). Not quite. Nearly.
MARY. There was such a handsome young man in the Piazza this morning, when I was feeding the pigeons. It's fun feeding the pigeons, isn't it? You can feel their hearts beating against your wrist. . . . Yes, he was handsome. Did you notice him?
JOANNA. Not particularly.
MARY. Wouldn't it be wonderful if we met some foreign prince . . .
JOANNA. Two princes.
MARY. All right. Met two foreign princes, and they fell in love with us . . .

4

JOANNA (*stoutly*). We'll have to make do with what we can get. And working girls don't marry princes. That's a story. It never was true and it never will be.

(*The midnight bell begins to chime.*)

MARY. Oh, I say, it is getting late! (*Turns; sees smiling* WAITER.) *Cameriere!*

WAITER (*coming forward*). *Si, Signorina.*

MARY (*her Italian very limited*). *Voglio la*—er . . . *la conta* . . . *prego.*

WAITER (*in good brisk English, picking up slip from tray*). Here you are, miss. All ready. (*His accent is slight and must on no account be exaggerated.*)

MARY. Oh, thank you! Do you speak English?

WAITER (*smiling*). Pretty well. Yes. I have lived in England.

MARY (*remorsefully*). I'm afraid we've kept you too late. You're wanting to close down.

WAITER. Oh . . . (*Waving his hands.*) In the season it is all hours. But now, the nights grow cold. There was snow in Padova yesterday.

JOANNA. *We* haven't felt cold!

WAITER. The magic keeps the cold out, yes? (*To* MARY.) The Signorina was whistling a very old song just now.

MARY. Oh! Do you know it?

WAITER. Everyone knows the tune. But not many know the words.

JOANNA. Do you know them?

WAITER. Oh, yes. *Certamente.*

JOANNA (*impulsively*). Sing them for us!

WAITER (*laughing*). Ah! You think because the Italians sing, *all* Italians sing. Many have voices like frogs. I have a voice like a frog. But this I will tell you: the song belongs to the legend.

MARY. What legend is that?

WAITER. The legend of the pigeon with the silver foot. It is a very old one. You were talking just now of princes who come to marry poor young ladies with no money . . .

(JOANNA *and* MARY *look shamefacedly at each other: giggle.*)

JOANNA. It was only fun.

WAITER (*leaning over table and preparing to address them*). There was once upon a time a *very* poor young lady called *Bianca*, a lacemaker, who lived behind the church of San Cassian. Now this young lady longed for a handsome lover . . .

(*The light fades and leaves the stage in darkness.* BIANCA'S *voice is heard singing. After the first verse of the song, the middle arch, representing her home, is brightly illuminated.* BIANCA, *a girl of sixteen, is examining the lace she has made during the day, and is singing rather sadly to herself. The tune of her song is the one* MARY *has been whistling. Her costume is roughly that of the mid-eighteenth century, but very poor and ragged. Her room, as stated, is bare but for a bed, a chair, and a small table, but on the last is a cheap but pretty cup of Venetian glass.*)

BIANCA (*sings*).
>Moon and waves of the white lagoon
> Are bringing my love to land,
>And the stars fade as my love flashes
> The ring on his milk-white hand.
>Serene he steps from the sill of the dawn
> And the smile that he saves for me
>Catches his eyes, as St. Mark's catches
> The sun across the sea.

(MARIO, *a young man,* 20 *or so, enters* R., *walks along arches and knocks at the lighted arch, which represents* BIANCA'S *door.*)

MARIO. Bianca!

BIANCA (*starting up*). Mario! How late you are! I was just going to bed.

MARIO. Aren't you pleased to see me?

BIANCA. Oh yes, of course, but . . .
MARIO (*stepping into the room and sitting down on bed*). But what?
BIANCA. I'm so tired! So tired!
MARIO. *Poveretta!*
BIANCA. It's been such a long, hard day. And all the days are the same.
MARIO. I know. You work too hard.
BIANCA. And my eyes are so sore from making the lace. You can't think how sore they are and how tired I am. (*Quickly.*) But I mustn't be selfish. Life is hard for us all, and your hands are blistered from the oars.
MARIO (*leaning forward and putting his hands on her shoulders*). My hands are healed again when I put them on your shoulders.
BIANCA. Let me go, please. I know what you've come to say. You say it every night.
MARIO. And I know what you say, too; but I shall never stop asking. Let us be married, Bianca, darling, and we can at least be poor and tired together, but have the fun of laughing together a little as well.
BIANCA. I can't, dear. We've been brought up side by side since we were children. We know each other too well. And besides . . .
MARIO. Besides, what?
BIANCA. You think I am silly.
MARIO. I could think you were the silliest girl in the world and love you just the same.
BIANCA. Well, then . . . I have a very queer feeling that my love is waiting for me. That he is very handsome and proud and rich, and that one day he will come and make me a lady.
MARIO (*laughing*). And what shall I do if he does?
BIANCA. You will marry Caterina, Bertolo's daughter. I have seen you look at her. You would make love to Caterina if you weren't so sorry for me. If you didn't feel bound to me.

MARIO (*indignantly, starting up*). What rubbish! I never looked at anyone but you.

BIANCA. I have seen you look sideways into Caterina's black eyes.

MARIO. They're not black. They're blue.

BIANCA (*triumphantly*). And you tell me you have never looked at Caterina!

MARIO. Oh! You're a terrible girl! You don't deserve a fellow like me. (*Trying to embrace her. Tenderly teasing her.*) Do you now? Tell me.

BIANCA. Neither of us deserves to have to marry the other simply because everyone says we ought to.

MARIO. Everyone expects it. And they all say: "Two can live as cheaply as one".

BIANCA. I don't want to live cheaply any more. I'm so tired of working that sometimes, when I get up in the morning and look at my lace, I wish it would turn to foam and that I was under the foam, just sleeping, and sleeping forever and ever.

MARIO. Oh, my pet! You mustn't say that.

BIANCA. How can I help it? It's so hard, when you're not very old, to do nothing but work and sleep even to get a loaf of bread. Sometimes I earn so little that I'm afraid I shall have to sell my beautiful cup.

(*She takes cup from the table and turns it lovingly in her hand.*)

MARIO. You love it, don't you?

BIANCA. It was the only present my mother gave me. And, of course, it's not worth very much, but it's pretty! (*Adoringly.*) Isn't it?

MARIO. Very pretty.

BIANCA. My grandfather was a glass-blower. He was poor, too, as we've always been, and had to sell everything he made except just this one thing, which he kept for himself. I always feel that so long as I have it I shall somehow be all right. But sometimes I'm frightened that even that will have to go—and then—I think I should die. (*Pause.*) And sometimes I feel I shouldn't be so sorry if I did. It would only be like going to sleep and not having to get up in the morning.

MARIO. Don't, my darling! You're only a child.

BIANCA. We are both lost children, both of us, and nobody cares about us, and nobody ever will, unless . . .

MARIO. Unless what?

BIANCA. I am right about my lover.

MARIO. Your handsome, rich, proud lover. Am I nothing at all to you?

BIANCA. If you would stop thinking about me you could marry Caterina Bertolo, whom you love, and Caterina's father would give you work in his boat-house, and you wouldn't be poor any more.

MARIO. Oh, be quiet about Caterina!

BIANCA. She doesn't interest you at all?

MARIO. Not at all.

BIANCA. She has a lovely voice, and sings very high.

MARIO. Very low.

BIANCA. She has little feet.

MARIO. Not so little as yours.

BIANCA. But pretty?

MARIO. Pretty-ish.

BIANCA. In her red shoes with the stars on the toes.

MARIO. They came from Florence, those shoes!

BIANCA (*laughs*). Oh, oh, oh!

MARIO. Why are you laughing?

BIANCA. Because you are so uninterested in Caterina Bertolo! Dear Mario, you must go now, because I am very, very tired and if I don't go to bed now I shall sleep till noon.

MARIO (*kissing her cheek before she can escape from him*). I shall come again tomorrow night and say all the same things.

BIANCA. No, dear: it's no use.

>(*She goes to the door to bid him good-bye, but at that moment a masked and cloaked lady,* THE CUSTOMER, *comes swiftly along the arches,* R. *She may, if practicable, be attended by two torch-bearers who take up their positions at either side of the arch during the following scene.*)

THE CUSTOMER (*in a sharp, authoritative voice*). Is this the home of Bianca, the lacemaker by the church of San Cassian?

>(MARIO *steps back into the room.* BIANCA *remains on doorstep.*)

BIANCA. *Gentilissima signora,* if you will please step in.

CUSTOMER. It will please me better if you will step out, and a little way out of earshot of this young man. The night is warm and I should stifle in your small room.

BIANCA. My room is small but clean, and the windows are open to the water.

CUSTOMER. If you please.

>(*She draws* BIANCA *out into* C. *of stage. The light follows them, leaving* MARIO *in shadow. He stands listening.*)

Now, signorina, I have a fancy to buy your lace. A handkerchief, only a handkerchief.

BIANCA. But I must fetch my lace to show you!

CUSTOMER. How shall I know better than you what is good and what is bad? You shall sell me the most beautiful handkerchief you have, with the linen no more than an inch square, and the lace a hand's breadth deep all round: and you shall not sell it for money.

BIANCA. Signora, it is by money that I live. I would like to give you a handkerchief, because it would be foolish of me to pretend that you are not the most grand, and I am sure, the most beautiful customer I ever had, but if you give me no money I shall have no breakfast.

CUSTOMER (*calling back over her shoulder*). Young man, fetch the girl a handkerchief, the finest of all.

BIANCA. But he doesn't know where to look! He doesn't understand at all about lace. He doesn't know the difference between Venetian point and a fishnet.

CUSTOMER. The first his hands light upon will be the finest. You shall see.

(MARIO *comes out with a handkerchief which he gives to* BIANCA.)

MARIO. Will this do? This was the first I saw.

(BIANCA *looks at it. Stares dumbfounded at him.*)

Isn't it all right?

CUSTOMER (*taking the handkerchief. To* BIANCA). You see? It is as I said. (*To* MARIO.) You are an amiable young man and I like your face, but you had better go home now. You have played your part and shall have your reward.

MARIO. But I don't understand.

BIANCA. Do as she says, Mario.

MARIO. I—oh, very well. (*Subdued.*) *A rivederla,* Bianca. I shall see you tomorrow. (*He goes off* R.)

CUSTOMER. He will not see you tomorrow because at midnight you will be feeding the pigeons in the Square of Saint Mark's.

BIANCA (*laughing*). But there are no pigeons in the square at midnight! They are all roosting in the spires and rooftops with their heads under their wings.

CUSTOMER. We shall see. (*She is putting the handkerchief away in her sleeve.*)

BIANCA. *Signora,* that will be one ducat.

CUSTOMER (*sharply*). I told you. I do not buy with money.

BIANCA. Then with what?

CUSTOMER. With a handsome, rich, proud lover.

BIANCA (*overcome with shame and annoyance*). Oh, you must have heard what I said to Mario! You must have been listening! I know—you were in your gondola beneath my window and you listened to it all!

CUSTOMER. My good girl, do I seem to you like a listener at

casements or keyholes? Really, I shall be out of patience with you.

BIANCA. Then how—

CUSTOMER. Be quiet and don't ask questions. If you want your lover, you will do as I say. At the end of every day you will buy a *schei's* worth of grain. Every night at twelve you will go to Saint Mark's Square and feed the pigeons. Many will come to you, but you must watch for the pigeon with the silver foot. And when the silver pigeon alights upon your hands, clinging to your fingers and pecking grain from your palm, your lover will come to you from the lagoon and make you his bride.

BIANCA. But I have no money for grain! I can hardly feed myself.

CUSTOMER. You have a little money saved for a rainy day and you shall spend it. Every night you shall go to the Square until the pigeons fly to you, but if one single night you fail— your lover will never come, and you will live in this hovel for the rest of your life.

BIANCA. But *signora,* how shall I believe all this?

CUSTOMER. Did you believe Mario would bring me the right handkerchief? To your bed now, and tomorrow, do as I say. (*She turns to go, turns back.*) There is nothing else you have to sell?

BIANCA. I have a great deal of lace.

CUSTOMER. Not lace. Something hard and bright that glitters on your table.

BIANCA (*stiffening*). That is not for sale.

CUSTOMER. Not for money?

BIANCA. Nor for a lover.

CUSTOMER. Are you sure? We shall see. Tomorrow in the Piazza at midnight. (*To torchbearers.*) Come!

(*She sweeps off* R. *and the light goes out. The* WAITER'S *voice is heard in the darkness.*)

WAITER. Now Bianca did not know what to believe or not to believe, but the more she thought about her strange customer the more she was tempted to do as the lady said, and see what would happen. So on the next evening she bought a little grain out of her tiny store of money so carefully hoarded, and set out for St. Mark's Square.

(*As he continues to talk, the light falls to the* R. *of the stage, and the scenes he describes are mimed by* BIANCA.)

She stood in the cool night with her palm out-stretched, looking upwards towards the domes of St. Mark's, that glistened in the moonbeams as if they were spread with fine snow. There was a smile on her face, a little unbelieving, a little bitter, perhaps, because she was afraid a joke was being played on her. But then the first pigeon flew down and clung to her fingers.

(BIANCA *must make her audience believe in the pigeons, which, of course, are not to be represented.*)

She gave a cry of delight, and stroked its wings as it picked away at the grain. She touched its little feet, but they were rosy-red in the moonbeams, not silver at all. And then the birds came flying from everywhere, beating about her shoulders, cooing against her cheeks. They flew upon each other's backs, struggling for a place upon her fingers, on her palm or her wrist or her arm, and she could not help laughing for sheer surprise, and because it was so funny to see them fight. With her free hand she pushed them apart, searching among beaks and feathers for the silver foot, but there was no silver foot.

And as suddenly as the birds had come they flew away, and all the grain was gone, and Bianca, with her hands empty at her sides, so very disappointed and sad, went slowly on her way back to her home behind the church of San Cassian.

JOANNA'S VOICE. Oh, poor old Bianca! I feel so sorry for her.

MARY'S VOICE. But it came out all right in the end, didn't it? I mean, she had a lover, only she didn't realize it, and—
WAITER. *Zitto, signorina!* You run on too fast. You shall hear what happened if you will be patient a little while longer. Next night the same thing happened, and again the next, and again and again, until . . .
(*The light goes up in the* C. *arch.* BIANCA *is sitting on the edge of her bed in tears.* MARIO *is sitting helpless at her side.*)
BIANCA. All my money has gone! I can't buy any more grain, not a single lentil. I can't even buy supper for myself.
MARIO. I wish I hadn't eaten mine. Not that it was much.
BIANCA (*wistfully*). What was it?
MARIO. Only a bit of bread.
BIANCA. With sausage?
MARIO. Well, only a little piece.
BIANCA. And wine? Did you have wine?
MARIO. Only a glass of wine. And the cheapest wine, too. You wouldn't have liked it. It was so sour.
BIANCA. I would have liked anything, *anything!*
MARIO. Oh, I am so sorry! The thought of my own supper chokes me. But you know, you'd have eaten, too, if only it hadn't been for those wretched pigeons!
BIANCA (*flaming up*). Don't say that! Don't you see what a miracle it was that they came at all?
MARIO. I expect you'd come running pretty quickly if anyone suddenly offered you a meal at midnight. Nothing wonderful about that.
BIANCA. Oh, I'm sure it's wonderful! You should have seen them. They came down in a great whirling cloud, and their feathers were all pink and green in the moonlight, like the glass my grandfather used to blow, and they came around my feet till I was paddling in a sea of pigeons!
MARIO. But they were just ordinary birds. None of your silver-footed sort. What a lot of nonsense you believe!

14

BIANCA (*starting up*). You're hateful, Mario! And you can go home. I don't want you here.

MARIO. Don't be so silly.

BIANCA. I mean it. Go home! Go home, do you hear? As if it isn't bad enough to be cheated and hungry, without being laughed at into the bargain!

MARIO. So you admit you were cheated?

BIANCA. Go away.

MARIO. If I go, I shan't come back.

BIANCA. Don't, then, don't! Go to Caterina Bertolo and talk your good, sound common sense to her! She'll like it better than I do. (*With dignity, showing him the door.*) A rivederla, Mario.

MARIO (*after a pause*). Addio. (*He makes her a sweeping mock bow and goes out into the darkness, R.*)

    (BIANCA *flings herself at full length on the bed, weeping, and kicking her heels. She is in a small tantrum of disappointment, and she is, indeed, dreadfully hungry.*

    The CUSTOMER *appears rather suddenly in the doorway, unattended or not, as the producer pleases. If the torchbearers are with her, they flank the doorway as before.*)

CUSTOMER. It is half-past eleven by the parish bell and you have not set out for San Marco.

BIANCA (*starting up*). You again! Oh, I don't want to be rude, *signora,* anyone will tell you I am never rude, but I wish I had never set eyes on you!

CUSTOMER. Rudeness doesn't bother me. Why have you not set out for San Marco?

BIANCA. Because I have no grain left.

CUSTOMER. Then buy some.

BIANCA. I can't. I have no more money. I haven't even enough to buy myself supper!

CUSTOMER (*impatiently, stepping into house*). Oh, you're a silly girl! You don't deserve a lover.

BIANCA. Why am I silly? Why should you call me silly because I have no money left? Money is easy for ladies like you.

CUSTOMER. You could find money.

BIANCA. How?

CUSTOMER. You have still something left to sell.

BIANCA (*eagerly*). If the *signora* would care to look at the veil I finished today, the finest net, so fine it would only be a shadow over her golden hair, trimmed with the most delicate *point de Burano*—

CUSTOMER. I do not want any lace. In my house I have coffer upon coffer of lace far finer than yours, all laid down in lavender. I will buy this. (*She takes up the cup.*)

BIANCA. That is not for sale! Not for a thousand ducats, *signora!*

CUSTOMER. I am not offering you a thousand ducats. I am offering you the price of one packet of grain.

BIANCA. I don't want any grain. I'm tired of pigeons and tired of your story-telling. I don't believe there is a pigeon with a silver foot.

CUSTOMER. It's strange that the birds come to you, though, is it not?

BIANCA. They're just hungry. As I am.

CUSTOMER. So you won't be going to the Piazza tonight? What a pity.

BIANCA. Why?

CUSTOMER (*dreamily*). Even now his gondola may be setting out over the sea. He may be lying even now on the cushions, trailing his long white hand in the water, his bright and sparkling gaze upon the shore and towers of Venice. I can almost see the small waves rippling over his ring. Listen.

(*Two or more female voices singing very softly*)

VOICES.   Moon and waves of the white lagoon
                Are bringing my love to land,
           And the stars fade as my love flashes
                The ring on his milk-white hand . . .
CUSTOMER. Two *schei* for your cup.
BIANCA *(torn)*. Oh, I don't know what to say!
CUSTOMER *(with authority)*. Two *schei*, and be off with you!
BIANCA *(sobbing)*. I wish I were strong enough to say no. But I can't! I can't! Give me the money, take the cup and go.
> *(She thrusts the cup into the* CUSTOMER'S *hand. The* CUSTOMER *gives her the money, bestows the cup under her cloak and goes swiftly away. Black-out of the scene.)*

WAITER'S VOICE *(in darkness)*. So Bianca ran off very fast indeed, very fast, so that she had to think about running and not about crying, and she ran through the little streets and the alleys and over the bridges but when she was half-way along the Mercerie,* an old woman sprang up in her path.
> *(Light shines on* R. *of stage.* BIANCA *and the* BEGGAR WOMAN, *shapeless in rags, are confronting each other. The* BEGGAR *has her arms flung wide, to stop* BIANCA'S *progress.)*

BIANCA. What are you doing? You mustn't stop me now.
BEGGAR. You must help me, pretty *signorina*, for if nobody helps me my grandson will die.
BIANCA. I can't help you. I don't know how. And I'm in a terrible hurry!
BEGGAR. He must have the yellow medicine from the chemist, or he will die. He is only ten years old. And I have no money to buy the medicine. Only two *schei*, *signorina*, only two *schei*!
BIANCA. I can't give it you—I can't! I have only two *schei* in the world and that is to buy me a lover.
BEGGAR. My grandson is only ten years old and he is gasping

*Pronounced "Mair-chay-ree-eh"

for breath. Lover or no lover, you are alive, and you see the sun rise in the morning over the lagoon, and you know how nice bread is to eat and water is to drink, but tomorrow he will see nothing and know nothing, for ever and for ever. (*She kneels at* BIANCA's *feet. Simply.*) Please give me the money. You are good and kind. You would not see a child die, not for all the lovers in Christendom.

(BIANCA *hesitates for a moment. Then with a sob and a gasp, she tosses her last two schei to the ground and runs off* L. *Black out.*)

MARY'S VOICE. The beggar woman was really the Customer, I suppose, testing Bianca out?

JOANNA'S VOICE. I always thought all this testing was rather mean, as a matter of fact.

WAITER'S VOICE. Yes, you are right, it was the Customer in disguise: and I agree this testing is, as you say, a little of a cheat. But as you saw, Bianca behaved very well indeed, and gave all her money away.

JOANNA'S VOICE. What did she do then? Just go off home?

WAITER'S VOICE. No. Somehow, she couldn't bring herself to go home. She felt she was so near the Piazza that she might as well finish her journey. So she stepped into the Square and it was blazing with the moon. You could have read a newspaper by the light of it. You could also see the smallest tear on Bianca's cheek. And the first thing Bianca saw was that she was not alone.

(*The lights go up on to stage* L. *The* LOVER *in black cloak, three-corner hat and the grotesque Venetian mask, the* bauta, *stands facing audience, his arm outstretched. He is feeding the pigeons.*

This scene is played both by him and BIANCA *in mime, according to the description of the* WAITER.)

In the middle of the square was a young man, handsomely

attired in tricorne hat and cloak, but she could not see his face, for he was wearing the famous Venetian mask, the *bauta*, which looks just a little frightening, don't you think? But the gallants of those days used it for a disguise when they were off to meet ladies whom they should not meet.

And the whole square was alive with pigeons, flying about the young man's head, so that now and then, laughing, he had to beat them away; covering his arm like a muff of feathers, ebbing and flowing in a feathered sea about his feet.

Bianca watched him, hands clasped upon her heart. Suddenly he spoke.

LOVER. Why don't *you* feed them, too?
BIANCA. I can't. I haven't any grain.
LOVER. Can't you buy some?
BIANCA. I haven't any money. I gave it to a beggar woman.
LOVER. Then I shall give you some of mine. Hold out your right hand.

(BIANCA *does so and he pours the grain into her palm; the miming action takes place as the female voices sing.*)

VOICES.　　Moon and waves of the white lagoon
　　　　　Are bringing my love to land:
　　　　And the stars fade as my love flashes
　　　　　The ring on his milk-white hand.
　　　　Serene he steps from the sill of the dawn
　　　　　And the smile that he saves for me
　　　　Catches his eyes as St. Mark's catches
　　　　　The sun across the sea.

(MIMING ACTION: *Young man moves slowly* D.S. *and stands with his arms folded, his back to the audience.* BIANCA *goes through performance of thanking him for the grain. She goes* U.S., *facing the audience and feeds the birds. First she kneels, encouraging them to come about her feet. One springs on to her finger. She rises very slowly from her knees, bearing the bird upwards. Then they crowd upon her.*)

BIANCA. Another, and another and another! I never saw so many!

LOVER. Look for the silver foot!

BIANCA (*excitedly searching*). Have you got it, you with the green breast? No. Rosy feet only. Have *you?* You're a fine bird, a prince of birds, very fat. No. Don't drive the others away, greedy! You're a pigeon in the manger. You don't want to eat yourself, do you? And you won't let your friends eat, either. You, now, come off my shoulder, so that I can see you! Ah, I believe it's you! Don't struggle, I mean to hold you tight—(*In tone of extreme disappointment.*)— No. Not you. Come on, come on, all of you . . . you, with the white cross on your tail, show me your foot. . . . No. (*Cries out.*) Oh! They've all gone, every one! Come back, come back! Oh, they mustn't leave me now, they mustn't, they mustn't . . . (*Weeping.*) I knew it would be no good, I knew, I knew. And they've all gone, and my grain is all gone.

LOVER. You have one last single golden grain clinging to your shawl.

(BIANCA *searches, finds it.*)

Put it on your palm. Hold it out. So. Now wait.

(*She stands quite still, her head raised, her palm outstretched.*)

SINGLE FEMALE VOICE (*singing*).
    Serene he steps from the sill of the dawn
    And the smile that he saves for me
    Catches his eyes as St. Mark's catches—

BIANCA (*crying out*). Look, here he comes!

WAITER'S VOICE. A single bird flew down from the spire of St. Mark's, circled Bianca's head, dropped lower and fluttered about her hand, not perching, not perching, not yet . . . feathers ruffled, eyes bright, not quite to be caught . . . then—
. . .

BIANCA. Ah! (*Her face is radiant. She watches the bird as it lights upon her wrist and pecks at the single grain.*) It has a silver foot! It is the pigeon with the silver foot! He's flying away now . . . oh, don't fly away now . . . oh, don't fly away, don't, don't . . .

> (*She stops short. There is a moment of complete silence. Then, as if compelled, she moves slowly towards the motionless young man.*)

BIANCA. Take off your mask.

> (*He does not respond.*)

BIANCA. Please. Please. Take off your mask.

> (*The* LOVER *raises his hands to his head. The mask falls at his feet.* BIANCA *can see his face, but the audience cannot.*)

(*Joyous.*) It is you!

> (*He opens his arms wide and she runs into them. He bends his head to kiss her, then sweeps his cloak around her, obliterating her from view.*)

SINGLE FEMALE VOICE.
>> And the smile that he saves for me
>> Catches his eyes as St. Mark's catches
>> The sun across the sea.

> (*Black out.*)

> (*The light goes up on the modern scene. The* WAITER, *smiling, is standing with his arms outspread, indicating that the story has come to an end. The girls, leaning across the table, propped on their elbows, chins in their hands, are gazing at him.*)

JOANNA. So it was Mario after all, who was the real lover all the time!

MARY. And she found what she needed in him, the moral being that what we most desire is often too close for us to see it.

WAITER (*after a pause; briskly*). Not at all. It certainly wasn't Mario.

JOANNA. } What?
MARY.

WAITER. He married Caterina, Bertolo's daughter, went into business and was happy ever after.

MARY. Then who was the man in the mask?

WAITER (*patiently*). The lover she'd been promised, of course, handsome, proud and rich. You think poor young ladies never marry princes, don't you? Well, usually they don't. But Bianca did. And if you take the *vaporetto* along the Grand Canal you will see, not far from the Ca' d 'Oro, to the left of it, the wonderful palace where they lived and died, always happy and always in love.
So there's hope for you, ladies!
Let me see . . . *trecento, quattrocento, cinquecento . . . sei cento*, if you please!

(MARY *pays him. The girls rise, collecting their guide-books and belongings.*)

Grazie, signore, buona sera, and I wish you a prince apiece, for you see, it *can* be done!

The girls laugh, nod to him and stroll slowly off arm-in-arm, R., MARY *whistling the song, as*

THE CURTAIN FALLS.

THE COPYRIGHT ACT, 1956

N.B. *Before any performance of this play can be given, application must first be made to* EVANS BROTHERS LIMITED *for a licence, and it is advisable that this should be done* **before rehearsals begin.** *Any performance of this play without a licence is illegal. For full particulars please refer to* COPYRIGHT NOTICE *on page two of cover.*

The Bauta

Oval Mask

COSTUME

This need only suggest the eighteenth century, except in the case of the LOVER, who must wear the traditional tricorne and *bauta*.

BIANCA. Long, full-skirted dress of some coarse material, grey or faded blue. Probably patched. A small woollen shawl, just covering shoulders.

MARIO. White shirt, tattered breeches to knee, red sash.

CUSTOMER. Long, full-skirted dress of some rich and shining material, orange or yellow. Hair dressed high, and black lace shawl arranged over head and flowing over shoulders. She wears a black mask—preferably the lace-edged, oval mask covering the centre of the face, as in paintings by Longhi.

BEGGAR. Black rags covering whole of head and dress and shadowing the face.

LOVER. Long-skirted coat, preferably of some brilliant material, emerald, red or violet, black silk stockings. Buckled shoes. Long black cape. Scarf swathed over head, with tricorne on top. The long-nosed white mask, concealing face to upper lip, the *bauta*.

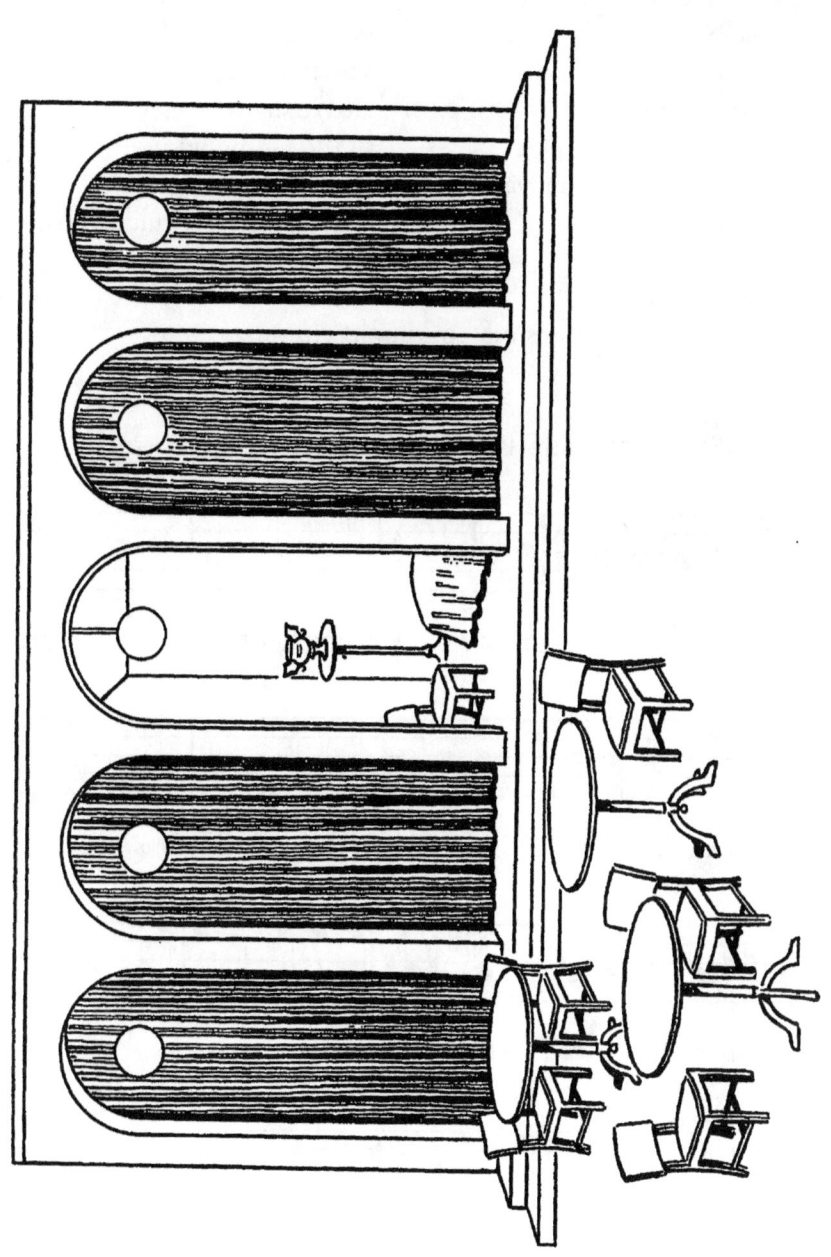

FURNITURE AND PROPERTY PLOT

On the Stage
Café tables and chairs
Bed, table and chair
Lace
Venetian ornament or vase
Ice-creams, ashtrays
Tray
Café bills

Personal
MARIO—a lace handkerchief
CUSTOMER—money
BIANCA—money
LOVER—bag of grain
MARY—money, guide books, camera, etc.

Noises off—midnight chiming

Song for 'The Pigeon with the Silver Foot'

Moon and waves of the white la-goon are bring-ing my love to land. And the

stars fade as my love flash-es the ring on his milk-white hand. Se-

rene he steps from the sill of the dawn, and the smile that he saves for me.......

Catch-es his eyes, as Saint Mark's catch-es the sun a-cross the sea.........

www.ingramcontent.com/pod-product-compliance
Lightning Source LLC
Chambersburg PA
CBHW061519040426
42450CB00008B/1692